Thank you, Lord, for the person that has decided to do the 30 day challenge to face any truth about themselves, whether good or bad. I pray that You (Lord) strengthen them and encourage them through this process in Jesus' mighty name.

Say out loud: "I will no longer allow the world to dictate my perception of what I see when I look into the mirror."

Now, go boldly in front of the mirror and say, "It's on, and I'm not backing down!"

www.mascotbooks.com

The Battle in the Mirror

For more information, please contact:
Mascot Books
620 Herndon Parkway #320
Herndon, VA 20170
info@mascotbooks.com

Library of Congress Control Number: 2020905016

CPSIA Code: PRFRE0620A
ISBN-13: 978-1-64543-366-8

Printed in Canada

As I look at my reflection in the mirror, I cannot forget about the people who have struggled with depression, had traumatic experiences, or endured sickness in their body that caused them to have changes in their appearance that directly impacted how they view themselves in the mirror. If this describes you, I offer encouragement toward taking the steps necessary to gain back your confidence in finding freedom and self-acceptance in the mirror. I dedicate this journal to you.

I also dedicate this journal to two important people who have continually brought inspiration to my life. My beautiful sister-in-law, Phyllis Elaine Williams (December 8, 1967—February 14, 2020), who throughout the years was my biggest cheerleader for writing this journal. Words cannot express how much her support meant to me. She blessed my life tremendously, and I thank God for her every day. And to my beloved grandmother, Maggie Collins, who was a strong woman known for speaking her mind. I thank her for helping me throughout her ninety-eight years of life to discover my own courage and inner strength to be the strong woman of God I am today. I love you forever, Grandma Maggie.

The Battle in the Mirror

A 30 Day Challenge

That Will Change the Way You See Yourself in the Mirror

Frederica W. Mercado

Foreword

The urge to write this journal has been in my heart for many years. I guess what I allowed to hold me back was the lack of courage. The courage to take the first steps, the courage to stop hiding and to come out of my shell. For many years I spoke about the concept for writing *The Battle in the Mirror*. I knew that one day I wanted to speak about the challenges and perceptions of self-image with my family, friends, and the world. Sometimes, I would feel this overpowering energy that would come over me and change my entire state of mind. It was like I suddenly would experience unspeakable joy from the inside at the thought that my experience could potentially have a positive impact on other people's lives. My inner self was rooting for me and cheering me on, pushing me to bring *The Battle in the Mirror* to existence, and finally, one day, I stepped out on faith and wrote this journal.

I began putting my thoughts down on paper by doing a self-evaluation of my life using my notes over the last twenty years in regard to my own "battle in the mirror." I was able to draw from my own personal battles of dealing with depression and not loving myself because of my perceived imperfections. For many years I would see things about my appearance when I looked into the mirror that were simply not true and struggled with the urge to not feed into those negative thoughts. I would ask family members if they noticed what I was seeing when I looked at myself in the mirror, in which they responded that they did not see the flaws I saw in myself.

During those years, I learned that my perception of myself was my own reality when I looked into the mirror. I further realized if I was the only one seeing me a certain way, then it was up to me to go back and pay attention to what I was thinking and re-examine what I was believing about myself. It has taken me many years to get my thoughts right, or to have right thinking about myself (as I call it).

Although I have felt a calling to write a journal for the last twenty years, I believe it was in 2011 that God clearly spoke into my heart about doing this 30 day challenge in the mirror. At first, I hesitated, but eventually I accepted the challenge because I wanted to get to the root cause of my thoughts. When I initially went to the mirror and documented my first thought about myself, it was nowhere near positive. At that very moment, I knew that my thoughts were betraying me, but I honestly couldn't begin to fathom how to change them. I believed and accepted just about every thought that came into my mind—the "good" and especially the "bad." Thank goodness that as my relationship with God grew stronger, I began to understand the difference between good and bad thoughts. I had no idea that my thoughts were defining, molding, and shaping me into the person that I was becoming. I am thankful to God that through many years of battling the mirror, I can now stand in front of the mirror and claim *victory* over my insecurities. Even as I age and start noticing the subtle changes to my appearance, I will continue to love myself and accept all of my imperfections and shortcomings. This feeling of self-acceptance was not accomplished overnight. However, I knew staying positive and committed to God's Word was more beneficial to my life than listening to my own self-sabotaging negative thoughts.

My desire for each person who decides to embark on this 30 day journey is that by the end of this challenge, you will have gained a better understanding of your doubts and fears. My sincere hope is that you will be able to reflect upon the areas where you have made a change in your life and that you would start to have confidence when you go in front of the mirror, so that each day you will have a little more freedom than the day before as you begin to like parts of you that you didn't like in the past and eventually wholeheartedly love and accept all of you. I pray that you will be rejuvenated by the renewal of your mind and that you will finally see what's been there all along: a beautiful child of God!

"Think about where you want to be in life,
and think about what it will take to get you there.
In the end, we all choose where we want to be.
We choose it by our actions or by doing nothing."

The Battle in the Mirror

What do you see when you look into the mirror? Do you see yourself as the Lord sees you? According to Psalm 27, we are the beauty of the Lord in the land of the living. God created us in His image (Genesis 1:27). So why are so many people feeling bad when they look into the mirror? Could it be that most of us are believing and accepting the lies of the world? As soon as you step in front of the mirror, there is an opportunity for "the lies" to begin.

And here are some examples:

> I really need to lose some weight, my face is too big.
> I don't like my nose.
> My teeth are too dull and crooked.
> I wish I was taller.

And the most powerful one of them all:

> I'm ugly. I wish I looked like this person or that person (but the truth is you look *exactly the way that God created you*).

Imagine that the mirror is the world looking at you, staring back at you, putting pressure on you to change who you supposed to be and to take away your self-worth. The truth is that we sometimes accept what the mirror (world) tells us about ourselves, whether positive or negative. And yes, we love the positive, as we should love it, but when we accept the negative and allow it to make us feel bad or bring us down, then we are opening up the door for self-doubt to enter into our lives. When we accept the perceived negatives about ourselves, we can become moody, lose our confidence, and most importantly, lose our sense of self-worth. We must remember that we are appreciated and valued as the righteousness in Christ Jesus created in the image of our Father. We must remember these things when we go to the mirror! We must take a stand against our negative thoughts! The good news is that we *can* change our perceived negative thoughts if we're willing to accept the truth about ourselves. If we can accept that we're not perfect, we can focus our time on the way God sees us! So, take a deep breath, exhale, and say, "I'm not perfect and never will be. I need to just accept it!" Now didn't that feel good? I hope it felt good and put a smile on your face, which is definitely the intent of this journal.

I pray over the next thirty days that you will find the courage to face your fears and doubts when you look into the mirror. I pray that as you go through this journey of strengthening acceptance toward all your faults and flaws, you will be empowered to look at yourself and adore the person in the mirror. I have faith that you will become what you believe about yourself if you can commit to putting in the work of self-love. So, let's get started.

New Beginnings
DAY 1

New beginnings can be a wonderful change in our lives—there's excitement and anticipation, along with feelings of nervousness. It's waking up knowing that you're going in a different direction or that you have decided to take a chance and trying something new in your life. For some of us, we try to imagine what it would be like when we finally reach that goal or finish that challenge; however, none of us can predict the future. So instead of worrying or being anxious, put your trust in God! By putting your trust in God, you can enjoy the journey of discovering who you are and how you truly feel about yourself when you go in front of the mirror.

Date _____

What do you see when you look at me?

When I first looked into the mirror, my first thought was:

_____

My next thoughts were:

_____

_____

_____

_____

_____

_____

_____

_____

_____

_____

_____

_____

_____

_____

_____

_____

_____

_____

_____

_____

Life Point: Your first thought when you look into the mirror is your most powerful thought. That first thought plays a big role in how you see yourself.

Encouragement: Don't allow yourself to feel bad about your thought process because this exercise is designed to help you change your thought process.

Say Out Loud: I am in the process of renewing my mind, and I am thankful to have God's grace and mercy upon me.

Scripture Adapted from (NIV) Job 8:7: Your beginnings will seem humble, so prosperous will your future be.

Cares

Day 2

As you reflect upon yourself, ask yourself the following questions: Are your looks the most important aspects of who you are? Do you love to look at yourself in the mirror? Do you decide how much you will like a person based off of their appearance? Do you choose your friends based on their looks? Did you choose your spouse or significant other based on their physical appearance? Do you care what other people think about you? If you answered "yes" to any of these questions, you're not alone. Most of us allow looks or physical appearance to determine at least one or most aspects of how we view ourselves and others. But we must remember that looks only represent our outward appearance, and we shouldn't make them the center of our lives.

Date _____

What do you see when you look at me?

When I first looked into the mirror, my first thought was:

_____

My next thoughts were:

_____

_____

_____

_____

_____

_____

_____

_____

_____

_____

_____

_____

_____

_____

_____

_____

_____

_____

Life Point: Place your cares on what's important in your life.

Encouragement: Don't allow looks to be the determining factor of how you base your decisions and choices in life when it comes to choosing friends, etc. As we age, beauty fades, and once it fades, then what?

Say Out Loud: I choose to care about the important things in my life. The rest is irrelevant.

Scripture Adapted from (KJV) 1 Peter 5:7: Casting all your care upon him; for he careth for you.

Worries

Day 3

How much time do you spend worrying about situations and circumstances in your life? How much time do you spend in the mirror thinking that you need to lose weight, or asking yourself how you will survive to the next payday? Worrying about a situation will not change that situation, it will only stress you out and consume you. In those moments that seem dire and without a solution, you must seek the Lord for His comfort and guidance and believe in your heart that He will make a way and provide for all of your needs.

Date _____

What do you see when you look at me?

When I first looked into the mirror, my first thought was:

_____

My next thoughts were:

_____

_____

_____

_____

_____

_____

_____

_____

_____

_____

_____

_____

_____

_____

_____

_____

_____

_____

_____

_____

Life Point: Worry doesn't add to your life, it takes away from your life. When you worry, it doesn't make you feel better and it doesn't change your situation. All it does is cause you to stress over the situation.

Encouragement: When worry starts to consume you, grab hold of it and cast it out of your life.

Say Out Loud: I trust You, Lord. I refuse to let worry consume me.

Scripture Adapted from (NIV) Luke 12:25–26: Who of you by worrying can add a single hour to your life? Since you cannot do this very little thing, why do you worry about the rest?

Judgmental
Day 4

Are you judgmental of yourself and others? Do you always find and point out the flaws in yourself and others? When you go in front of the mirror, are your first thoughts telling you what's wrong with you? Do you accept those thoughts? Do you entertain them? If you said "yes" to any, or all of these questions, you're not alone. Many people have those struggles; however, you can vow to make a change in your life today by making a commitment to stop accepting and entertaining those negative and judgmental thoughts about yourself. Turn your thoughts around by making a decision to uplift, edify, and encourage by speaking positive words over your life and others.

Date _____

What do you see when you look at me?

When I first looked into the mirror, my first thought was:

_____

My next thoughts were:

_____

_____

_____

_____

_____

_____

_____

_____

_____

_____

_____

_____

_____

_____

_____

_____

_____

Life Point: When you go in front of the mirror, decide to make a change by taking off those judgmental eyes and replace them with eyes of compassion.

Encouragement: Don't allow yourself to judge others; you can stand against it and defeat this spirit of judgement.

Say Out Loud: I will not be judgmental toward myself and others today.

Scripture Adapted from (AMP) Matthew 7:1: Do not judge _and_ criticize _and_ condemn [others unfairly with an attitude of self-righteous superiority as though assuming the office of a judge], so that you will not be judged [unfairly].

Jealousy
Day 5

When you look into the mirror, are you disappointed or jealous because your face or body doesn't look like someone that you know or admire? As a result, do you start to dislike your own appearance, and do you get the desire to spread untruths about the person (that you secretly want to be like or look like because you are jealous)? Why do so many women feel like they have to tear down another woman to make themselves feel better? Make a decision today to not be that kind of woman, and remember no matter how many modifications you make to your appearance, *you will still be you.* So, embrace all the inner and outer beauty God blessed you with and do not envy any other person.

Date _____

What do you see when you look at me?

When I first looked into the mirror, my first thought was:

_____

My next thoughts were:

_____

_____

_____

_____

_____

_____

_____

_____

_____

_____

_____

_____

_____

_____

_____

_____

_____

_____

_____

Life Point: Tearing down another woman with your words will only make you feel better for that moment. The fact of the matter is that you still have to go back in front of the mirror and look at yourself. Then what?

Encouragement: Don't give in to the temptation of jealously. Remove yourself from the situation and go do something positive.

Say Out Loud: Thank You, God, that I'm willing to face the truth about myself, so that You can help me deal with my insecurities.

Scripture Adapted from (AMP) I Corinthians 13:4: Love endures with patience *and* serenity, love is kind *and* thoughtful, and is not jealous *or* envious; love does not brag and is not proud *or* arrogant.

Enough
Day 6

Have you ever looked into the mirror and said that you have had enough of a particular situation? That you are not going to take this anymore, or that you're not going to stand for this anymore? That you desperately need for a change to take place in your life? I believe there comes a time in all our lives when we all have said "enough" to a particular situation. Everyone's breakthrough is different, but it could come from us standing in front of the mirror, finally coming to the realization of the pain we have endured, and making the decision that it ends today. We may have to cry, scream, or talk to God about our thoughts and fears, but before we walk away from the mirror, we have a plan—a plan for how we will handle what is to come knowing that He is in control.

Date _____

What do you see when you look at me?

When I first looked into the mirror, my first thought was:

_____

My next thoughts were:

_____

_____

_____

_____

_____

_____

_____

_____

_____

_____

_____

_____

_____

_____

_____

_____

_____

_____

_____

Life Point: Once you're at the point of enough, you have opened the door for change to enter into your life.

Encouragement: Take control over whatever you have had enough of. Once you take control over it, you take back your power.

Say Out Loud: I take control/power over _____. I now rule over it, and it will never rule over me again, In Jesus' mighty name.

Scripture Adapted from (KJV) Luke 10:19: Behold, I give unto you power to tread on serpents and scorpions, and over all the power of the enemy: and nothing shall by any means hurt you.

God's Plans

Day 7

We all make plans for our lives. Some of us even write them down and feel confident that these are "my plans," and all I have to do is follow them and watch my desires come to life in the exact order I wrote them down. Sometimes they do, but what happens when your plans don't work out the way that you planned them? How do you respond to that?

Date _____

What do you see when you look at me?

When I first looked into the mirror, my first thought was:

_____

My next thoughts were:

_____

_____

_____

_____

_____

_____

_____

_____

_____

_____

_____

_____

_____

_____

_____

_____

_____

_____

_____

_____

_____

_____

Life Point: Remember that situations and circumstances change, but the Lord changes not!

Encouragement: Even if your plans don't work out the way that you wanted them to, you should never give up on your dreams. Pray about them and seek God for how you can align your desires with His will. Even if you have to start over, don't give up, because Jesus is on your side.

Say Out Loud: God has a good plan for my life, and I believe that I'm walking in His will for my life daily.

Scripture Adapted from (AMP) Jeremiah 29:11: "For I know the plans *and* thoughts that I have for you," says the Lord, "plans for peace *and* well-being and not for disaster, to give you a future and a hope."

Who Am I?

Day 8

Who are you when you're in front of the mirror? Do you practice your fake smile and your fake laugh with your fake voice? Or better yet, do you practice your fake cry? Who are you trying to be when you look into the mirror? Or whom are you trying to fool? The truth is, you can't fool yourself, and you definitely can't fool God. How about this: try keeping it real by being yourself. God formed you with His hands when you were in your mother's womb. He knew you before you were born. Your purpose comes from Him, so remember nothing you do is a surprise to Him, your Creator.

Date _____

What do you see when you look at me?

When I first looked into the mirror, my first thought was:

_____

My next thoughts were:

_____

_____

_____

_____

_____

_____

_____

_____

_____

_____

_____

_____

_____

_____

_____

_____

_____

_____

_____

_____

_____

_____

Life Point: It takes a lot of energy being yourself, so why waste it trying to be someone that you're not?

Encouragement: God doesn't see us and our imperfections. He sees us through His Son Jesus Christ, and He sees us as the righteousness of Christ.

Say Out Loud: Something good is going to happen to me today!

Scripture Adapted from (AMP) Isaiah 64:8: Yet, O Lord, You are our Father; We are the clay, and You our Potter, And we all are the work of Your hand.

Righteousness

DAY 9

When you stand in front of the mirror, you must remember that you have been clothed in *righteousness.* You have a robe of righteousness upon you. You are in right standing with the Lord. By knowing who you are in Christ, you won't be easily deceived by the lies of the world. You are fearfully and wonderfully made. So, smile and embrace the fact that God loves and cares about you.

Date _____

What do you see when you look at me?

When I first looked into the mirror, my first thought was:

_____

My next thoughts were:

_____

_____

_____

_____

_____

_____

_____

_____

_____

_____

_____

_____

_____

_____

_____

_____

_____

_____

_____

_____

_____

Life Point: God is your everything, and apart from Him, you would be completely lost.

Encouragement: It's your God-given right to life and a relationship with Christ. You just have to ask Him to come into your life and have faith He's working on your behalf.

Say Out loud: I am the righteousness of God in Christ!

Scripture Adapted from (AMP) Isaiah 61:10: I will rejoice greatly in the Lord, My soul will exult in my God; For He has clothed me with garments of salvation, He has covered me with a robe of righteousness, As a bridegroom puts on a turban, And as a bride adorns herself with her jewels.

Obedience

Day 10

Have you ever said, "I'm going to save up for a special occasion?" Or, "I'm going to stay on track this year and get my health or my finances in order?" But instead you are steadily spending money and eating a lot of unhealthy foods. And before you know it, your bank account is low because you are spending a substantial amount of money on eating out and shopping, and now you realize that your bills are due and your credit cards are max out. Then you start to feel overwhelmed because you realize that you have not followed one item on your "list." If this happens, you must remember that you can change the whole process of not being disciplined if you place boundaries and seek God for guidance on how He can help you stay on His chosen path for your life. It may take a while to see changes in the areas you desire, but do not give up! It may be hard at first, but you can do it! With faith and obedience to God, He can completely change your circumstances.

Date _____

What do you see when you look at me?

When I first looked into the mirror, my first thought was:

_____

My next thoughts were:

_____

_____

_____

_____

_____

_____

_____

_____

_____

_____

_____

_____

_____

_____

_____

Life Point: Messing up or making mistakes are a part of life. As long as we learn from those experiences, we will continue to grow as a person.

Encouragement: Even if we mess up, trust and believe that God will give you plenty of chances throughout your lifetime to get it right.

Say Out Loud: Thank You, Lord, that through Your grace and mercy, I will get another chance to get it right.

Scripture Adapted from (AMP) 2 Corinthians 10:5: We *are* destroying sophisticated arguments and every exalted *and* proud thing that sets itself up against the [true] knowledge of God, and we *are* taking every thought *and* purpose captive to the obedience of Christ.

Freedom

Day 11

Freedom to focus on our personal appearance is a gift and a privilege that we sometimes take for granted. We don't give a second thought when we go to the bathroom and look into the mirror to make necessary adjustments. But imagine if that was taken away and you had no mirror to look into, or that you were too afraid to look at yourself in the mirror. Due to an illness that has drastically changed your perception of your appearance, could you imagine the last time you looked in a mirror being the last time you would ever see yourself? How would you feel?

Date _____

What do you see when you look at me?

When I first looked into the mirror, my first thought was:

_____

My next thoughts were:

_____

_____

_____

_____

_____

_____

_____

_____

_____

_____

_____

_____

_____

_____

_____

_____

_____

_____

_____

_____

Life Point: Whether you spend a lot of time or a little time when you go in front of the mirror, remember your freedom to do so.

Encouragement: Always remember to be thankful and grateful for what you have, because there's someone in this world praying for what God has already blessed you with.

Say Out Loud: Thank You, Lord, that I will not waste this day complaining about what's wrong with me; instead, I will exercise my freedom and just be thankful.

Scripture Adapted from (AMP) John 8:36: So if the Son makes you free, then you are unquestionably free.

Understanding
Day 12

Do you understand how important it is for you to accept yourself when you go in front of the mirror? To accept all of you? To understand that God Himself formed and created you in His image? When He sees you, He sees *perfection* because He's looking at you through the eyes of His son, Jesus. So why can't we see ourselves the same way? Can you accept your image today and every day, to promise to love yourself from head to toe? What's stopping you?

Date _____

What do you see when you look at me?

When I first looked into the mirror, my first thought was:

_____

My next thoughts were:

_____

_____

_____

_____

_____

_____

_____

_____

_____

_____

_____

_____

_____

_____

_____

_____

_____

_____

_____

Life Point: What you see in the mirror is your own perception, and what you believe about yourself is your reality. Change your thought process and you will change your perception about yourself today and every day of your life.

Encouragement: Trust and believe that God is working in you to help you see yourself as He sees you.

Say Out Loud: God's power is working in me right now so that I will see myself as He sees me.

Scripture Adapted from (NIV) Proverbs 4:7: The beginning of wisdom is this: Get wisdom. Though it cost all you have, get understanding.

Change
Day 13

Change can be difficult, uncomfortable, and comes with drawbacks. However, we need change, and without it, we would most likely remain stagnant and never grow. Without change we could potentially remain in that same area of our lives for weeks, months, or even years. God could be calling you into a different season of your life, but in order to seize the opportunity of growth, you must be willing to change. If this is the case for you, you can use each opportunity as a learning tool to help you realize areas in your life where you want God to help you. I encourage you to speak change into existence and to believe that you're going to step into the next chapter of your life with unspeakable joy and favor. In Jesus' mighty name.

Date _____

What do you see when you look at me?

When I first looked into the mirror, my first thought was:

_____

My next thoughts were:

_____

_____

_____

_____

_____

_____

_____

_____

_____

_____

_____

_____

_____

_____

_____

_____

_____

_____

_____

Life Point: Change your thoughts, and you will change your destiny.

Encouragement: Change is a process that takes time. Allow change to work in you, and one day you will look back on your life and be thankful for it.

Say Out Loud: I believe that I can change, and I am ready for change to take place in my life. It may be difficult, but I fully accept and embrace it.

Scripture Adapted from (KJV) Romans 12:2: And be not conformed to this world: but be ye transformed by the renewing of your mind, that ye may prove what is that good, and acceptable, and perfect, will of God.

Forgiveness
Day 14

We all need forgiveness in our lives. At certain times we are called upon to forgive, and other times God uses people in our lives to forgive us. It's so important to understand that the act of forgiveness is liberating. When we hold on to unforgiveness, it keeps us captive, and it reminds us of all the reasons why we shouldn't keep holding on to the resentment. Sometimes we hold on to unforgiveness likes it's a newborn baby: we cradle it, we rock it, we keep it hidden away in our hearts for days, months, years, or in worst cases, to the grave. The longer we hold on to it, the longer unforgiveness has time to make us bitter, harden our hearts, and control our thoughts. If this is the case for you, I pray you will declare victory over it! As you look into the mirror, search your heart. If you find the spirit of unforgiveness, make a decision today to release it and forgive in the mighty name of Jesus.

Date _____

What do you see when you look at me?

When I first looked into the mirror, my first thought was:

_____

My next thoughts were:

_____

_____

_____

_____

_____

_____

_____

_____

_____

_____

_____

_____

_____

_____

_____

_____

Life Point: Holding on to unforgiveness can change you. It does exactly as it says, "It keep us captive." It may even control you if you decide to give in to it. Does it?

Encouragement: Take a deep breath and celebrate in the mirror your new-found freedom from unforgiveness.

Say Out Loud: I forgive myself for being so hard on myself, for comparing myself to others, for not being perfect, and most importantly, for putting pressure on myself for holding on to _____.
Thank You, Lord, that I release all of that pressure, and I am now _free_.

Scripture Adapted from (AMP) Ephesians 4:32: Be kind _and_ helpful to one another, tender-hearted [compassionate, understanding], forgiving one another [readily and freely], just as God in Christ also forgave you.

Hope
Day 15

Do you ever go to the mirror and hope that situation weighing you down and causing you to have headaches and stress would just disappear? If that happens, do you just want to escape and focus on something positive for the rest of the day? I think we all try to focus on those moments of hoping for something better and wanting something good to happen to us or our family. Just remember that each day we have a choice of where, or in whom, we decide to place our hope. By placing your hope *in the Lord*, you are placing *your hope* in something positive and everlasting. So, make the choice today to continually place your hope in the Lord, you won't regret it!

Date _____

What do you see when you look at me?

When I first looked into the mirror, my first thought was:

_____

My next thoughts were:

_____

_____

_____

_____

_____

_____

_____

_____

_____

_____

_____

_____

_____

_____

_____

_____

_____

_____

_____

_____

_____

Life Point: There are millions of things or people that we can choose to place our hope in each day. I pray that you place your hope in God. By doing so, it lets the Lord know you trust Him.

Encouragement: Start placing your trust in the Lord; it will be the best decision of your life.

Say Out Loud: I hope for the rest of my life that I will know my self-worth when I look into the mirror.

Scripture Adapted from (AMP) Psalm 130:5: I wait [patiently] for the Lord, my soul [expectantly] waits, And in His word, do I hope.

Blessed

Day 16

Do you believe that you're blessed? You probably hear people say that phrase all the time, or maybe someone has even told you that you're blessed. The truth is, whether you choose to believe it or not, you are blessed. Life is a gift; each day is a blessing, and each day is filled with choices. You can make the choice to believe that you're blessed or not to believe you are blessed. I encourage you to stand in front of the mirror and speak blessings over your life concerning all things or all matters of your life. Start today by opening your mouth and declaring blessings over your life in Jesus' mighty name!

Date _____

What do you see when you look at me?

When I first looked into the mirror, my first thought was:

_____

My next thoughts were:

_____

_____

_____

_____

_____

_____

_____

_____

_____

_____

_____

_____

_____

_____

_____

_____

_____

_____

_____

Life Point: Each day you wake up is a new start, a new beginning, and I encourage you to make the most of it.

Encouragement: Use your words to build up and edify your life at all times. Start speaking blessings over your life today.

Say Out Loud: *I am blessed. You cannot mess with the blessed!* I have the blessings of Abraham upon me. Success has no choice but to come into my life!

Scripture Adapted from (KJV) Galatians 3:14: That the blessing of Abraham might come on the Gentiles through Jesus Christ; that we might receive the promise of the Spirit through faith.

Favor

Day 17

When you stand in front of the mirror, do you pray for favor? Or did you even know you could pray for God's favor in all things? God hears even the smallest of requests. You could say, "Lord, help me to have a good hair day. Help my hair stay in place." Or if you have experienced difficulties with growing your hair, you could say, "Lord, help my hair grow. Lead me to specific products that will help it grow." Even if you have no hair due to illness, you could say, "Lord, I will not be ashamed of my appearance today." God hears all prayers, and you don't have to go through this journey of life alone. Seek Him and declare favor in all areas of your life today. But always remember, you don't have to pay attention to your flaws when you look into the mirror, especially when there are plenty of positive attributes staring back at you.

Date _____

What do you see when you look at me?

When I first looked into the mirror, my first thought was:

_____

My next thoughts were:

_____

_____

_____

_____

_____

_____

_____

_____

_____

_____

_____

_____

_____

_____

_____

_____

_____

_____

Life Point: Every day, pray for God's undeserving and extraordinary favor to be upon your life.

Encouragement: Pray for favor at all times, when looking into the mirror, getting a haircut, driving in traffic, standing in line, interviewing for a job, etc. God's favor has no boundaries.

Say Out Loud: I have the favor of the Lord upon me, therefore I am blessed in all situations, at all times.

Scripture Adapted from (AMP) Ephesians 4:7: Yet grace [God's undeserved favor] was given to each one of us [not indiscriminately, but in different ways] in proportion to the measure of Christ's [rich and abundant] gift.

Love

Day 18

Choose to love yourself, choose to love others, and choose to love freely with a genuine heart. Most of us find it hard to love ourselves and others. We convince ourselves it's someone else's fault and say things such as, "They shouldn't have done something to anger me." The truth is that most of us find it easier to love others if they act the way that we want *them to act.* We base our love off of conditions, such as choosing friends based off their appearance, how they dress, or different aspects of their background. As a result, we begin to love people only if they meet our conditions, ultimately showing conditional love instead of unconditional love. However, wouldn't it be wonderful if you decided to love yourself just as you are, and to love others just as they are? Make a conscious decision today to remove any conditions you may have toward yourself and others and decide to love unconditionally.

Date _____

What do you see when you look at me?

When I first looked into the mirror, my first thought was:

_____

My next thoughts were:

_____

_____

_____

_____

_____

_____

_____

_____

_____

_____

_____

_____

_____

_____

_____

_____

_____

_____

_____

Life Point: You can't give away what you don't have. If you make a decision not to accept God's love, then you make it difficult to love yourself and others.

Encouragement: Start loving yourself today, just as God always has!

Say Out Loud: I choose to love myself and to walk in love today and every day for the rest of my life.

Scripture Adapted from (NIV) 1 Corinthians 13:13: And now these three remain: faith, hope, and love. But the greatest of these is love.

Joy
Day 19

How joyful are you when you look into the mirror? Do you have inner joy? The kind of joy that shows you're happy all the time, or you're simply happy for no reason? The kind of joy that makes you smile at everyone all the time? Even if you don't feel like you have that kind of joy, don't give up! Believe that you are filled with God's joy and that He is working on you today and at all times. Remember, God promises His children unspeakable joy. It is up to you to claim it and receive it in Jesus' mighty name!

Date _____

What do you see when you look at me?

When I first looked into the mirror, my first thought was:

_____

My next thoughts were:

_____

_____

_____

_____

_____

_____

_____

_____

_____

_____

_____

_____

_____

_____

_____

_____

_____

_____

_____

Life Point: Joy will change the atmosphere when you walk into a room. When you're filled with joy, you can't help but smile and be joyful. Joy is contagious, so be determined to spread it everywhere you go.

Encouragement: The joy of the Lord is your strength. He will grant you strength for any battle.

Say Out loud: I have God's unconditional joy inside of me, and I'm going to embrace it and spread it wherever I go.

Scripture Adapted from (AMP) Nehemiah 8:10b: And do not be worried, for the joy of the Lord is your strength *and* your stronghold.

Peace

Day 20

Do you have peace when you go in front of the mirror? Are your thoughts all over the place, racing through your mind and letting you know everything that you need to fix in your life? Are your thoughts telling you to give up? Or do the same thoughts keep repeating themselves in your mind, like a record on repeat? If you said "yes" to any of these questions, it could be because your thoughts are attacking you, putting pressure on you to act on them even if it means doing something that you know is not in God's best interest for your life! However, what's important to remember is that you don't have to accept those thoughts. Take a deep breath and start speaking positive thoughts over your situation and life right now! If you have to go in front of the mirror and speak back to the negative thoughts, then do it. Pray to God about leading you to spiritual resources or Godly counsel if needed. Remember, you are not alone, and it is okay to work toward maintaining a peaceful life.

Date _____

What do you see when you look at me?

When I first looked into the mirror, my first thought was:

_____

My next thoughts were:

_____

_____

_____

_____

_____

_____

_____

_____

_____

_____

_____

_____

_____

_____

_____

_____

Life Point: If you are struggling with maintaining your peace, seek God and pray for it to return ten times more. Remember, God is always with you and wants the best for your life.

Encouragement: Believe that you're making progress each day and that each day your faith will grow stronger.

Say Out Loud: Thank You, Jesus, for Your perfect peace that You have bestowed upon my life. I accept and choose to live a good life.

Scripture Adapted from (AMP) John 14:27: Peace I leave with you; My [perfect] peace I give to you . . . My perfect peace calm you in every circumstance and give you courage and strength for every challenge.

Confidence

Day 21

Confidence is a choice that you have to make each day. No matter what your current situation is, only you can choose to be happy or unhappy. You can choose to be confident in all things, even when you go in front of the mirror, or in incidences when you are having a bad day. Have confidence in the fact that God is working in your life and He is able to change any situation. When you place your confidence in God, it brings joy and increases the chance of you having a great day. You should remember once you choose to put on confidence, don't allow anyone or any circumstances to convince you to give it away. It belongs to you, so wear it like a badge of honor.

Date _____

What do you see when you look at me?

When I first looked into the mirror, my first thought was:

_____

My next thoughts were:

_____

_____

_____

_____

_____

_____

_____

_____

_____

_____

_____

_____

_____

_____

_____

_____

_____

_____

_____

Life Point: Wear your confidence as a badge of honor, and it will lead you down your path to your God-given destiny.

Encouragement: Don't allow anyone to take away your confidence; it's yours for life. Remember, it can only be given away, but never taken.

Say Out Loud: I am confident in all things. Thank You, Jesus!

Scripture Adapted from (KJV) Philippians 1:6: Being confident of this very thing, that he which hath begun a good work in you will perform it until the day of Jesus Christ.

Rest

Day 22

Are you always tired when you look into the mirror? Do you have rings or dark circles under your eyes? It could be a sign of a lack of proper rest. Proper rest is crucial to your mind, body, and spirit, and lack of rest could affect your ability to excel and to focus on God's purpose for your life. Our bodies were created to take a break and relax, because without proper rest, we increase our chances of becoming irritable and moody. Make a decision today to put rest at the top of your priority list. Your body will thank you for it.

Date _____

What do you see when you look at me?

When I first looked into the mirror, my first thought was:

_____

My next thoughts were:

_____

_____

_____

_____

_____

_____

_____

_____

_____

_____

_____

_____

_____

_____

_____

_____

_____

_____

Life Point: Without proper rest it is difficult for our immune system to make all of the repairs that our bodies need to recover.

Encouragement: Sometimes we get busy with life. It happens; however, just remember it is okay to *not* say, "yes" to everything and everyone. Put some time aside and say, "yes" to your body.

Say Out Loud: I am not going to feel guilty for making sure that I take care of myself and get the proper rest that I need.

Scripture Adapted from (AMPC) Matthew 11:28: Come to Me, all you who labor and are heavy-laden *and* overburdened, and I will cause you to rest. [I will ease and relieve and refresh your souls.]

Restoration

Day 23

Have you ever looked into the mirror and thought that you looked tired, even though you just experienced a good night's rest? Or you woke up the next morning with your mind racing all over the place and you felt like you had lost your peace of mind? If you have ever felt this way, you must remember that God is a God of restoration, and He can restore us if we place our trust in Him. He will not abandon us. He is our heavenly Father, and He wants nothing more than to restore our lives and to make us whole. Have faith that God will take care of you and restore you in all areas of your life.

Date _____

What do you see when you look at me?

When I first looked into the mirror, my first thought was:

_____

My next thoughts were:

_____

_____

_____

_____

_____

_____

_____

_____

_____

_____

_____

_____

_____

_____

_____

_____

_____

_____

_____

_____

_____

_____

Life Point: God knows how important your appearance is to you, and He is always working in our lives to help us through life.

Encouragement: Continue to live a healthy, balanced life, which includes making time for self-care on a daily basis.

Say Out Loud: My youth is renewed like the eagle's!

Scripture Adapted from (KJV) Psalm 103:5: Who satisfieth thy mouth with good things; so that thy youth is renewed like the eagle's.

Beauty
Day 24

Am I beautiful? When you look at yourself in the mirror, does that thought ever cross your mind? Do you ever tell yourself that you're beautiful? Or do you tell yourself all of the reasons why you could never be beautiful? Whether you believe it or not, you are beautiful and wonderfully made. God doesn't make mistakes, and He made you into His image, so embrace that thought and every inch of you because God loves you just the way you are! So, start today by telling yourself that you're beautiful, and most importantly, make a decision to believe it!

Date _____

What do you see when you look at me?

When I first looked into the mirror, my first thought was:

_____

My next thoughts were:

_____

_____

_____

_____

_____

_____

_____

_____

_____

_____

_____

_____

_____

_____

_____

_____

_____

_____

_____

_____

_____

Life Point: Physical beauty can never compare to inner beauty. Inner beauty is priceless!

Encouragement: Continue to work on your inner self, and it will reflect on the outside.

Say Out Loud: I am the beauty of the Lord in the land of the living. God loves me; therefore, I choose to love myself.

Scripture Adapted from (AMP) Proverbs 31:30: Charm *and* grace are deceptive, and beauty is vain [because it's not lasting] but a woman who reverently *and* worshipfully fears the Lord, she shall be praised!

Smile

Day 25

When you look into the mirror, do you smile? Do you show your teeth when you smile? You need to believe that you have a beautiful smile, and when you smile, it radiates joy and happiness. Even if you don't feel like it, still continue to smile, and eventually you'll start to feel better about yourself. Have you ever heard the saying that smiling is contagious? Well, keep smiling, and before you know it, others will be smiling back at you.

Date _____

What do you see when you look at me?

When I first looked into the mirror, my first thought was:

_____

My next thoughts were:

_____

_____

_____

_____

_____

_____

_____

_____

_____

_____

_____

_____

_____

_____

_____

_____

_____

_____

_____

_____

_____

_____

Life Point: There's power in your smile—the power to brighten up someone's day. Choose to use your power!

Encouragement: Smile when you look into the mirror. It will make you feel better about yourself and will energize you from within.

Say Out Loud: I'm not going to let the mirror (world) dictate to me what I think of myself. I choose to love myself every day knowing that I'm the apple of God's eye.

Scripture Adapted from (CEV) Proverbs 15:13: Happiness makes you smile; sorrow can crush you.

Laugh Out Loud
DAY 26

Are you ashamed to laugh out loud due to fear of what others will think about you? Well, don't be, because laugher is healing! Laugher brings joy, and a good laugh can even bring tears of joy. You do not want to look back on your life and realize that you have never laughed out loud because of fear of judgement. You should try it now in front of the mirror. You have nothing to lose, and you may enjoy it!

Date _____

What do you see when you look at me?

When I first looked into the mirror, my first thought was:

_____

My next thoughts were:

_____

_____

_____

_____

_____

_____

_____

_____

_____

_____

_____

_____

_____

_____

_____

_____

_____

_____

_____

_____

_____

_____

Life Point: Even the Lord enjoys a good laugh. He gave us the gift of laugher, and you should never silent it.

Encouragement: Make a choice to include laughter in your day.

Say (Laugh) Out Loud: I'm going to laugh often and out loud because the joy of the Lord lives in me.

Scripture Adapted from (AMP) Psalm 37:13: The Lord laughs at him [the wicked one—the one who oppresses the righteous], For He sees that his day [of defeat] is coming.

Pleasant Words

Day 27

When you go in front of the mirror, do you ever speak pleasant words over your life? Do you ever speak pleasant words about others? If you don't, it's not too late to start. You should try it right now, and from this day forward, you should include it in your daily routine in front of the mirror. Speaking these positive affirmations could change the outlook of how you see your life and destiny.

Date _____

What do you see when you look at me?

When I first looked into the mirror, my first thought was:

_____

My next thoughts were:

_____

_____

_____

_____

_____

_____

_____

_____

_____

_____

_____

_____

_____

_____

_____

_____

_____

_____

_____

_____

_____

Life Point: By speaking pleasant words over your life, you will build your confidence and add joy at the same time.

Encouragement: Most of us are not used to speaking positive words over our lives. Make an effort to start today and continue to make it a daily part of your life.

Say Out Loud: I enjoy my time in front of the mirror. I own the mirror; it doesn't own me.

Scripture Adapted from (AMP) Proverbs 16:24: Pleasant words are like a honeycomb, Sweet *and* delightful to the soul and healing to the body.

Patience

Day 28

How many of us have prayed for patience? At some point in the day, most of us have probably asked the Lord to grant us patience to deal with our kids, boss, traffic, spouse, or other aspects of our lives that we are having a hard time dealing with. However, sometimes circumstances are beyond our control, and we are placed in situations that we do not have control over. In these moments, we must learn to exercise patience, knowing that each time we are put in those situations, we become a little less irritable. There will be plenty of opportunities in our lifetime to display patience. You must remember that you are only in control of your own life, so you must not allow those circumstances to control your peace.

Date _____

What do you see when you look at me?

When I first looked into the mirror, my first thought was:

_____

My next thoughts were:

_____

_____

_____

_____

_____

_____

_____

_____

_____

_____

_____

_____

_____

_____

_____

_____

_____

Life Point: You will have many opportunities to exercise patience in your life; however, try to not allow those circumstances to control your peace.

Encouragement: Do yourself a favor: slow down and enjoy the moments of your life.

Say Out Loud: Lord, help me to display patience in every situation that I encounter today and every day.

Scripture Adapted from (KJV) Isaiah 40:31: But they that wait upon the Lord shall renew their strength; they shall mount up with wings as eagles; they shall run, and not be weary; and they shall walk, and not faint.

Dream Big

DAY 29

Have you given up on your dreams? Do you remember as a child all of the big dreams you had for your life? But to this date, for whatever reason, they have not yet been fulfilled. As a result, you give yourself a hard time about it by constantly telling yourself that you're a failure and it's too late for your dreams to come true. Well, I'm here to tell you that it's never too late! Make a conscious decision to go after them and pray for God's guidance. Pray that He will lead you down the right path to accomplish them, if it is in His will for your life. Remember, they are your dreams, and you can do it!

Date _____

What do you see when you look at me?

When I first looked into the mirror, my first thought was:

_____

My next thoughts were:

_____

_____

_____

_____

_____

_____

_____

_____

_____

_____

_____

_____

_____

_____

_____

_____

_____

_____

Life Point: If you don't believe in yourself, it will be hard for others to believe in you. You must press forward. No matter your age or circumstances, if there's breath in you, your dreams can come true!

Encouragement: God is your biggest cheerleader, and He will never give up on you.

Say Out Loud: I will never give up on the dreams and visions that God has placed inside of me. I believe that they will come to pass, and I will live out my dreams.

Scripture Adapted from (AMP) Galatians 6:9: Let us not grow weary _or_ become discouraged in doing good, for at the proper time we will reap, if we do not give in.

Future

DAY 30

When you're standing in front of the mirror, do you ever imagine what you will look like in five, ten, or even twenty years into the future? Do you say to yourself, "Will I age well? Will I look like my mother? Did my mother age well? Will I have wrinkles? Will I keep or dye my gray hairs?" The truth is that only you can answer those questions about yourself. But I pray that through your journey over the last 30 days, this exercise has taught you to look at yourself in a different way, through the eyes of Jesus Christ.

I hope that you will boldly look back and say that you're so thankful for accepting the 30 day challenge because it forced you to face some realizations about yourself that helped you become a stronger and more confident woman. And because of it, you opened up your heart and mind to accept and love yourself. So, here we are on day 30, and you're standing in front of the mirror hopefully smiling because you no longer have anxieties or doubts when it comes to your perception of yourself. You have been emboldened with faith and power, and your future is looking bright! So, smile and say in front of the mirror, "Bring it on, Future, because I'm ready!"

Date _____

What do you see when you look at me?

When I first looked into the mirror, my first thought was:

_____

My next thoughts were:

_____

_____

_____

_____

_____

_____

_____

_____

_____

_____

_____

_____

_____

_____

_____

_____

_____

Life Point: Use each day as a stepping stone for the next and believe that it will propel you into your future destiny.

Encouragement: Believe that your future is bright and that your latter days will bring even more than you could have ever imagined.

Say Out Loud: I made preparations for my future, and I trust God. Therefore, I will not worry about my future.

Scripture Adapted from (AMP) Proverbs 31:25: Strength and dignity are her clothing *and* her position is strong and secure; And she smiles at the future [knowing that she and her family are prepared].

Final Words

Even to this day, I still have moments when I struggle in front of the mirror. But I have learned to believe the good instead of the negative thoughts. As long as there's breath in me, I can stand each day in front of the mirror and declare that I will continue to place my faith and trust in the Lord. I have finally realized that if I truly love and accept myself, it won't matter what others or the world thinks about me. Each day I will walk with a little more freedom and confidence than the day before, and for that, I am forever grateful for the path that led me to face and *overcome* "the battle in the mirror."

Lord, thank You for guiding me over the last 30 days. I'm stronger, more confident, worthy, and powerful. More importantly, my life has changed, and I'm never going back to the place where I used to be. I thank You, Lord, in Jesus' mighty name, that I now have freedom in the mirror.

Prayer of Salvation

I believe that Jesus is the Son of God and that He rose from the dead on the third day. I ask that you come into my life and be my Lord and Savior. Thank you, Lord, for coming into my life and for saving me. Amen . . .